Ecotones

ECOTONES
JANET KAPLAN

THE **BLACK SPRING**
PRESS GROUP

First published in 2022
An Eyewear Publishing book, The Black Spring Press Group
Grantully Road, Maida Vale, London w9
United Kingdom

Typeset by User Design, Illustration and Typesetting, UK
Cover art by Janet Kaplan

The author has requested the publisher use American spelling
and grammar wherever possible in this edition

ISBN-13 978-1-913606-89-3

For my mothers and fathers, sisters and brothers.
Again and always for Ethan.
And for my new life, with all Hallelujahs.

TABLE OF CONTENTS

ECOTONES AND TEXTUAL CONVERGENCES

An ecotone [from "ecology" and the Greek *tonos,* "tension"] is a place where habitats intersect and converge; where, as examples, a forest comes to a meadow, a meadow merges with marshland, or a marshland edges the sea. In 'Life on the Edge,' her *New York Times* Op-Ed piece of 27 December, 2013, Akiko Busch extends the definition of an ecotone to refer to a place where past and present converge. I have followed Busch in extending the definition, here to mean a page on which past and present, poetry, fictional narrative, and scientific and historical texts intersect and converge.

I/   PLASMA

Manus tuæ fecerunt me, et plasmaverunt me.

–from Psalm 118:73, the Vulgate Bible

Your hands have made me and formed me.

PROLOGUE

Night's bauble, night's pixel
changes form

GOOD LIVING

Who are born ice

> The living and working rooms must be well
> ventilated. A window in the bedroom should
> be opened a foot both at the top and bottom in
> winter, twice as much when the weather is not
> cold Good food Business solutions About our
> ads

    air melting them like thoughts
    leaking space
    and leaky time

The older boys shove you and the boy you like between the
vestibule door and wall. Bronx side-street, late afternoon.
They make you kiss, say they'll pull your shorts down if you
don't. *I have asthma*, says the little boy, red-faced and wheezing.
Later, upstairs: shame's home and invisibility. Its permanence.

        Light—
        it licks
        the bright yolk
        the mind
        the drip

To live now, aware of permanence and its access to irony.
Take plastic, waste it into an ocean. Light breaks it to its
molecular soul. Invisible, it enters the plastic body.

> Exercise, especially such as calls into action the
> chest muscles and fills the lungs with air Some
> results have been removed *Watch,*

now he's getting ready! There he goes! Gee whiz!
Wasn't that swell?

Alvin Davidson,
The Human Body and Health, Revised
American Book Company, 1909

Woolner Calisch,
"Richmond Air Show of 1909"
Richmond-Times Dispatch, 1939

HELLO

Orchard Beach and blanket throngs. Wandering off meant trailing
wet sand-edges, shoreline's glare and shriek. Kids, gulls. Beyond
the jetties, rocky pools. Stand of trees. Heading back, you lose
them—sleeping mother and the father. Transistor's ballgame voice,
red-black thermos of gin.

A softness undone, harsher than fear: they're drunk, never noticed
you were gone—belying your lost-ness. But here they are,
sunlight's knives. Their acceptance of your nothingness.

Forget this world and all its troubles and if possible its
multitudinous Charlatans—everything in short but the
Enchantress of Numbers

```ada
with Ada.Text_IO; use Ada.Text_IO;
procedure Hello is
begin
  Put_Line ("Hello, world!");
end Hello;
```

Charles Babbage
on Ada Lovelace
England, 1843

Ada Language
developed by Jean Ichbiah
for the U.S. Dept. of Defense

LINEAR TIME

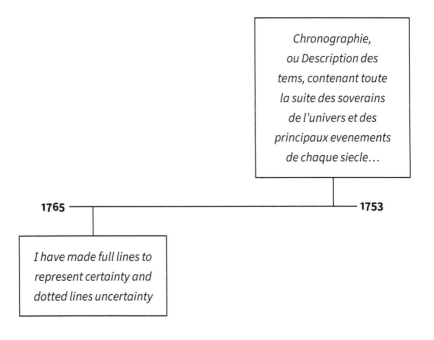

> Chronographie,
> ou Description des
> tems, contenant toute
> la suite des soverains
> de l'univers et des
> principaux evenements
> de chaque siecle…

1765 ——————————————————— 1753

> I have made full lines to
> represent certainty and
> dotted lines uncertainty

Present: nowhere
Past, set and certain: God
Your future, uncertain: Devil

Jacques Barbeu-Dubourg,
Chronographic Machine, timeline of
history beginning with Biblical creation
France, 1753

Joseph Priestly, *A Chart of Biography*,
graphing the lifespan of famous thinkers
England, 1765

TIME SURVEY

Wikiquick   time juiced   sticky

                with transgress—

                                              undressing

fluidity of clever siliconian bowels

                                   unpeeling like a latchkey kid
                                                   speedshock

        Him touching you there:

Didn't expect anyone home until dark   *warm bit of yourself—*

                                              and his tongue draws blood

                                ...

Some servers serving tiny specks of glottogony
                        language a lifestew monster
                                                         covers blown back
of time too complex   made of

a thief's thieved parts   leaking protean nucleic acids   ordure
in caves   unbreakable   ore of

cavernous hunger

clustered by rivers

wheels'
silk-plagued road

conquistadorial spillage
of sugar slaves

combustible

<lookinside!>
ceci n'est pas une vache

. . .

carbs

<blocks of twelve>

and *amaizeing*

pump powered
the slosh

. . .

tools in proto-human hands

Easily domesticated   caloric meat
biblically bitumenical

cooling the counting system
iron empires   scrawled-on treetrunk <codex>

gunpowder-compassed
ninetyfivepercent decimation rate

sugary coal up from ancient ferns
engines   exploiting

tional warring fare code   of now's molecular   interna
       ing   strophe strife matter's

crystal display unloved bits   earthlife a liquid
      earth a preverbal child's

  long memory

<*search* 'source': About 3,250,000,000 results (0.34 seconds)>

<*search* 'touch':

THIS BODY, THIS BLOOD

It had happened before—
but when, you didn't say.

Forced now to think about your body—
no more simple songs: armaments were out,

they were loose.

How much they weigh, you think—
those viruses, my errors.

A religious feeling comes to statistics   physical-textual imper-
manence to plasticity   polystyrenics to eternity's infinite house.

plasma   *homo plasmatos*

... each began to assemble
his forces for battle

Gonzalez de Clavjo,
Embassy to Tamerlane
Castile, 1403–1406

ORDER

Not a pleasant sound—   *Barefoot?*

Incredulous.   *Barefoot?*

You were a child, playing contentedly
on the sidewalk.

Drunk.   *Put yer shoos ahn.*

March. Before I—

Now exit the site,
not seeing what happens
when you go back inside.

Sunlight's orders: *feed yourselves and decompose—*. Meanwhile,
a seabird, alcoholic-like, fills itself with plastic.

Ordering Ordering Following
Ordering Food Online Birth Order
Ordering Fractions Ordering
If I were to follow your advice
how could I show my face…?
No, come what may tomorrow,
I must march

Ala-ud-Din Khilji, second ruler
Turko-Afghan Khilji dynasty
India, 1299

LIGHT, LESSER LIGHTS
<Precor hoc cape cara Volumen>

Lucens, Queen,
wrote Domnizo, a feeble monk,
Precor hoc cape cara Volumen
—as if to say *Take this precious book*

in which I write your blazing story
in the burning century that weds you
to humpback and stepbrother,
torch-lights the cells, the day's walled rule.

Unqueasy artist,
scale your length of world,
defeat worlds, install worlds—
and I, bit player, confessor-chronicler,
will write it

—as if to say *Take me;*
the sight of you doth eclipse my sight.

Your cunt tastes better
than whiskey,
your lover once said.
Then better with whiskey.

Then the whiskey had him.

Sunlight breaks the lesser codes
<a polymer or fuzzy note
that little time and light bits wrote>
and overwrites them with its own

Domnizo, *Vita Mathildis*

(Matilda of Canossa; Mathildis Lucens)

ca. 1115

KNOCK-KNOCKS

In a dark night

employ a chamber with a two-panel door...

bring several lamps

Add a thousand doors—or years—

set at different points in front of the door

and guess:

The experimenter should enter the chamber

close the door

leave a small gap between the panels

What moves

and observe the wall opposite the door

like prison walls in a dark night

further and further from sight?

You caught *A Clockwork Orange* at Film Forum. It sickened you—
overly-lit. *He allowed my wickedness*, you claimed. You were having
an affair; he just didn't want to guess.

Ibn al-Haytham, *The Book of Optics*
(written under house arrest)
Cairo, 1011–1021

BREAKING DOWN

Exclamation breaking onto the screen,
Onto the brilliant screen—a jackhammer!

Oh, the autumn foliage
Of the hill of Kamioka!

.   .   .

The sleeves of my coarse-cloth robe
Are never for a moment dry.

Then the back and forth with yourself:
Interview on a gravel hill.

.   .   .

No, they said. *No college.*
Who'll marry you if you go?

electrons→electric current→
a method to stun<erase>farm animals

.   .   .

→a treatment that sometimes cures
<erases>

Years later you said to your child: *If you go,*
who in hell will look after me?

After photo-decomposition—breaking down—plastic particulate
is too small to be seen.

from a waka attributed to
Empress Jitō (Unonosarara)
Japan, 703

HARMONY

Those Bronx Bundists,
they liked arguing

Grandfather—regular babysitter—had no
patience for Bundists, even less for Americans.
Women, girls, educated men. *Pah! Feh!*

weak coffee   *mushroom barley*
used napkins   *two-cents plain*

Old men in workshirts, coarse trousers,
suspenders. Their caps stayed on their heads.
They frightened you but you were among them.

Warm potato smell, Concourse lamplight through
plate glass, clatter of coffee-stained cups up from
the washers' steam. Unlonely saucers and cups.

It was harmony,
I'm telling you

Harmony is to be valued
and the avoidance of
wanton opposition honored

Prince Shotoku, from the
Seventeen-article Constitution
Japan, 604

MYSTERY

fecerunt me   *plasmaverunt me*

In commercial use since the year of your birth: bisphenol A.
It was, you thought, a message syringe.

fecerunt me   *plasmaverunt me*

that subject which is the greatest
mystery, which perplexes
the minds of the writers of
astronomical works, viz.,
the eclipses of the sun,
I am going to explain

Varahamihira,
The Panchasiddhantia
India, 575

IN RESIDENCE

devils = mailer daemons? let us not follow the opinion of some commentators and suppose him to be either the Devil or some demon but rather one of the human race in whom search human race...we should therefore concur that at the end of the world when the Roman Empire is destroyed there shall be ten kings who will partition the then an insignificant eleventh king shall arise search eleventh A Scandinavian classic that's perfect for elevenses or teatime Outerwear Military Green $407 Why did I get this ad of the human race in whom the Devil wholly taking up residence Parents finally dead, your younger brother kept the house—returned to it after work each evening as he'd always done. Bolt-locked himself into his own small room as he'd always done.

Saint Jerome,
Commentary on Daniel
Rome, 407

BODY POLITIC

Then we wrote lyrics praising you and you liked them.

Then we spent some time shooting arrows.

You gave me gifts:
a mulberry bow
and silver inkstone.

Then we became Person instead of persons,
each secretly wanting the Voice
of other voices

as at a fortuitous hunt,
a party of dignitaries and hounds—

no thicket, no covert, just a prized
fenced-in bird we'd have easy

In truth you liked the disposable: syringes, tubing tied tight for
a vein, Crazy Straws your husband used in your bongs—and,
later, lids burped onto Baby's Sippy cups and leftovers. Order.
Convenience. You envied the ease with which they fit, shaped to
perfection for every innumerable use, discarded without reflection.

You liked them, echoed the bird

Emperor Liu Cong to the
former, deposed Emperor
Huai of Jin, China, 312

NOSTALGIA

You Return

drunk at the screen
naked on a couch

swarming the window
flies want to get in
then out

Passing Out, You Drop the Screen

there, there   *no there*   *there*

there runs what is called a stream
which gives off a noxious stench…

…the city will benefit if it is covered.

Letters, Pliny the Younger,
governor of Bithynia-Pontus
109–111

DRINK

Some say
he split the object
to heal the split

      some think
      it's just language

           and some who are thirsty
           drink

                You'd never know
                which substance
                changed you

        thismybody
        thismyblood

And some plastics undergo
photo-decomp within a year
of entering the water.

                He pounded on the stone
                floor of the prison…
                splitting the stones and
                sending forth a spring

                    Jospers website,
                  on the imprisonment of
                  St. Peter in Rome, ca. 67

NIGHT

What was there to complain of but
that she had been loved?

—and the one whose name
means Darkness of Night:
did he look back—or did
the dark place look forward?

The grief-stricken birds,
the host of wild creatures, the
flinty rocks and the woods

never loved→unloved→dis-loved→matter yielding

You're lost and say
you want to go home, saying it steadily
to the child you've woken—

and with a flashlight you search.

So you arc towards yourself, invisible
as the unloved place from which you'd come.

Ovid, *Metamorphoses*
Rome, 8 AD

KNOWLEDGE

Who wants more words—tethered dogs, truckling! If you hold
them this time, it'll be to string them along, a chain extending quite
a way; though some damage should be expected from such long use

and later, as you
think around it,
you see that each
bit of dying
—as it gluts,
as there grows
more of it than
of yourself—
wants to be
remembered,
forevering
its blank screen-
captures,
recording its
simple white
messages over
your small dark
life

an ever-
expanding past
emptying itself
into you
as though
the brain were
a vast field with
a surfeit of Now;
and this glutting
and emptying,
as you think
around it, works
like the sun
as it lights
indiscriminately—
though some of us
burn

Concerning Knowledge:
Here and Now Be Humble—You Yourself!—in this Basement!
or peace and quiet will flee

Inscription (oldest evidence
of written Phoenician),
sarcophagus of Ahiram,
Phoenican King of Byblos
ca. 1,000 BC

IF THEN

If
a man's slave-woman,
comparing herself to her mistress,
speaks insolently to her,
her mouth shall be scoured
with one quart of salt
If
she's thirsty *<immen><tarsa><tersesthai>*
if she spoke   she heard   she scoured   if she missed
<skipped><mourned><fate-fatal-error>
childhood—if hers was salt
well then
she was born to
swallow herself dry
And if
baby bottles, formula packaging
<water pipes><DVDS><thermal paper sales receipts>
<touch, taste>
well then,
say Laws, bisphenol A
in food
too

Law 25
Ur-Nammu Law Code
Sumer, ca. 2050 BC

@WORK

>>>>— pictograph barley ca. 3011 BC
>>>>— barley cake
>>>>— cuneiform barley ca. 2900 BC
#you mustn't keep writing to me, you wrote to
your child
>>>>— it wasn't nostalgia, longing wedging open
time: it was their job
>>>>— we mustn't consider it an act of love
>>>>— this tablet records a quantity of barley
#when I was young, you wrote, grownups fought
all the time
#later, we tried to love, even when it was work
#even when it was work, we tried to stop
#I'm very sick now. I don't have time for you
>>>>— scribes had to account for the barley
>>>>— every sheath brought in as tax for the king

explosive plasma   light quanta to molten core   even at bottom—
light exists   seafloor to abyssal   midnight to twilight   sunlight to
garbage-island suspension   your home to   someone else's   I-thou
to *they*

>>>>— they had to keep tabs

Mesopotamia,
2900–3011 BC

ALTERNATIVES

bit <binary digit> equivalent to the result of a choice between two
alternatives

to overturn the appointed times　　　　　　　*to obliterate the divine plans*

aeonic thought bit or

unsearched search engine bit

silentspace bit or

sharp sharp　　　　　　　　　　　　　　　　　　　*sharp sharp*

logo-apple with a bite bit

plastic bit or

storms gather to strike like a flood bit

Moving van—you here? <*yes or no*> Did they keep her
notebooks? Were their swaddled bundles taken to the
cart? Planes along the new flight path. Screenlight.
Do they wake you? Did they wash a thousand birds?
For how long did they lament? Do you want to save
this? Does space <bitten place> want its bite back?
<*yes or no*> Whole again. Without us again.

The Lament for Sumer and Urim,
ca. 2900 BC

PLASMA: ANYTHING FORMED,

molded, image, figure… a piece of wax-
work…; of figures made by bakers,
cakes of incense…the body, as fashioned
by…counterfeit, forgery…; figment,
fiction…; of a story which is fictitious
but possible…; pretence… delusion

calculations
in syntax dressed

disquiet
armed and forward-marched

its voice
<multiple, singular>

piped into the ear
<as if up from a marsh>

and pumped into the eye,
a refraction

open mouthed,
a brief drink and inhalation

II/ CHRONICLES

LIKE CHRONICLE

And what is it like to be a bat?

Not *like* anything.

★

She unadorns herself, comes home to what she learned first.

        But you're like *me.*

I'll write about difference.

★

At first I felt like nothing. Wasn't here. Then I was, without your
knowing.
It felt like absence.

This is a presence. *Is.* But already I'm feeling *like* something.

I'm sorry to have you here like this—that you have to be here,
like me.

SMALL CHRONICLE

1.

When you're not, you can say you're small, say it next to something or someone smaller. Sit here, next to me. I'm sitting next to someone small.

2.

I don't know how you can bear to be alone with us.

3.

But you might not feel as small as you say you do, which means I'm alone again in my smallness.

4.

I'm a small person. I'm told all the time: You're not a small person. That you're here doesn't mean I'm not small. (Proof: no one knows you're here.)

5.

There were people smaller than I was, but they were happy. I wasn't. Not because smallness bothered me; only my smallness bothered me. It's what you mention first.

6.

You're important to me, you say.

7.

You want to be important to everyone but someone still dies, drooling and dribbling, no one to pluck long hairs from her chin.

8.

It's good no one has to see this except nurses and orderlies, for whom it isn't anything. But now it's possible *you'll* see, which doesn't do much good.

How is she?
Not so good.

(Not-So-Good Chronicle)

9.
She continues to think of herself this way, without being specific. Specifics let you think you see something.

10.
I was always told to speak up, speak clearly.

Don't swallow your sentences.

11.
Asked to clarify.

For example?

12.
We want to like it.

13.
It can't be liked, but it persists.

14.
That's seeing it clearly.

WRITING CHRONICLE

It hurts. You think, it hurts. You read, it hurts. You write,
no hurting, then resume. Hurt isn't writing. Hurt doesn't
do pleasure.

I'm tired of being moved by writing. Ads for being moved.
It's no one's fault, the writers are just doing a job. I read, I'm all
for it, I'm moved, I want it. I'm a gullible mess. Give it here.

No movement of its own, no authenticity. A forgery. Like being
stillborn but sucking the breast anyway.

Go back far enough, you'll find someone writing: *God isn't writing
this—I am!*

I'm fabricating this story!

DREAD CHRONICLE

Obviously, this low mood's what I have. Nothing else, just a low mood. It isn't even an authentic low mood, but I didn't acquire it by reading about other people's low moods. I could say it's mine, in this body I trust the mood's having a nice stay in.

Dread's here too. I was told, *Don't be alone, it's bad to be alone.*

Also: *I'm here.*

I was never alone. Dread came to make me be with people.

Dread knows about the void, silence. Low moods turn away; dread rarely rejects. Find a way out of *this* one. Dread was first to love the earth. It's authentic. It loved the animals, the people. It loved all their stories about it. It's possible that anyone who can love dread knows God.

Nothing that happens to me / in me is my doing. I can't take credit. Go puzzle over phenomena. Better yet, sit and watch:

The Dread Show—or, The Silence Chronicle.

(The Silence Chronicle)

Out there, the planet you wanted, inhabited by aliens who aren't showing up.

A story read to you the day you were born: Dread growing old alone. One day they'll shut up.

The large child arrives to demand credit. Will it ever get enough? Never. Nothing can appease it, the universe's steady whine, so small in the silence.

DYING CHRONICLE

In me, the thing I was born to do, taking place. I get to watch.
I wasn't awake for the construction but I'm here for this.
Fascinating! Until—.

Everyone knows pain's destructive unless, as everyone says, it cures.

To be cured isn't to not die, but to watch.

REPETITION CHRONICLE

Every day, I'm asked to repeat the corpse I was yesterday.
To consider dead things and feed them.

This will be dead soon, but now we're living: It feeds me, I feed it,
it feeds me, I feed it.

Now it's done. Why repeat myself?

Memories of memories, in their last throes, begging to be spared.
Keep going!

I've been afraid of dead and dying things. *Resurrect us!* they
cry from scratchy little throats. They pile up in insect mounds,
dry sticks twitching. They want to stay on, they want to be fed.

I was afraid of repeating myself, but I wanted to live forever.
A sideways loop ∞ appeared in the marketplace. *I'm an endless
repetition!* it said. Think of two round mirrors facing one another.
Stand between us.

How exciting to see so many me's!

In infinity, the repetitions can't be seen but they're there.
They're eating.

IMPOSSIBLE CHRONICLE

A boy was discovered not far from human interaction: good homes, an art school, love, all of which had eluded him. This happens but usually we don't hear about these children. They don't all grow up powerful and deadly, they don't all commit suicide in bunkers.

Decades later someone wanted the impossible to happen and so considered a man, an impossibly advanced man—he couldn't really exist, that's how advanced he was—coming upon the boy, bringing him home. *This is a very special boy*, he says to his impossibly advanced wife.

They tend to his needs, never take their eyes from him. They give him drawing materials, encouragement, a dog. They bend over him with love.

Then we all stop being and never were.

INTERNET CHRONICLE

Sometimes the internet's a mental hospital, zeroes in one wing, ones in another. You can't imagine there's anything meaningful. But that's family.

I dreamt about the Internet. *Far vhus is diss hinternet?* Grandma asked. We can go there if you like. She never came back.

Death, text me here!

I thought about the Carl Sagan movie, how they download instructions for a space module and Jodie Foster's character gets to see her father again—or a digitized him. The others think she's mental.

A voice was left with two digits, and with them it wrote to infinity. There's nothing else it can teach us, not with any variation of the sequence.

Lost, crazy, I follow the digits, babbling like a baby. To connect! To be inter! To be net!

Friends and faces, pages and birds. Grandma preferred her snake plant, her fine-toothed comb. I inherited them although I wanted her zeroes and ones. Hers in particular. I want them ad infinitum. Connected, as promised.

ACTING CHRONICLE

I'm interested in the performer. How does she feel up there,
in character?

Somebody who wants attention comes to the stage and asks why
I asked that.

The performer's so angry she won't look at us. Does she think she's
being ignored?

She's invisible, performed here by somebody else.

AX CHRONICLE

1.

Whenever it rains, I want to take a bow. It's clapping at something, isn't it? Rain's manipulated. It's got to rise, fall, make a sound.

2.

It's swirling, muddied, full of toxins. It should take an ax to the frozen sea, which is Kafka describing the act of writing.

3.

Something falls, something writes it down. Don't forget to take that bow. What would life be without a little narcissism, a go-cart that toots?

4.

Fyodor Mikhailovich Dostoyevsky knew that Ivan Fyodorovich Karamazov wasn't well; he warned us. Finally, Ivan himself knew. And so, when the devil visited again, Ivan thought it possible to say *It is I myself who am speaking, not you!*

5.

But you can't kill narcissism, Lizzie, not even with an ax. A narcissist learns there's nothing to give up. Ideas are so much chopped liver, but I'm still here. An image in a mirror or surveillance monitor. Making eye contact, I can tell you nothing noetic's going on.

6.

That ax. It's so cold in space, says the devil—or Ivan—all you'd have to do is touch the ax and your finger would fall off. And would it be possible for there be an ax in space? *What would happen to an ax in space?* Ivan asks. His guest is speechless. *Quelle idée!*

7.

The shoe, the one that's about to drop. I'd like to think of it as
a seasonal occurrence—spring, say, when if we're lucky the small
rain down does rain.

8.

Or both shoes, falling, falling. Ark-worthy, the pair of them.

9.

It isn't three in the morning, no one's here with *delirium tremens*.
But left and right are modified tomatoes, exploding sand,
cow farts hastening the catastrophe. Who can understand
the difference between narcissism and responsibility?

10.

Phases of the moon. A new one stares awhile, hooks a plane. Things
don't think of themselves as ritualistic, but I used to. I counted on it.

11.

Better not to know what's coming. Flowers, tears, pills, sentences.
For at least one person I know, those were last year's seasons.

12.

Baby crawling across the sand, loose socks, a happy ship. If he's
going to fall from that swing again, I'd like it to be in color, not this
black and white that says Fact!

13.

A rainy story, part of a child's leaky passage. When things can be
explained rationally, when they seem known, when a narrative
develops—radiation on the beach-umbrella's stripes—or notions
of progress. When he sees 'his life.' Another victim.

14.

An ax in space? *Quelle idée! If it went far enough it would, I think,
begin to orbit the earth, itself not knowing why....*

INVENTION CHRONICLE

A mechanism keeps me awake; it wants to invent things. We don't need anything else.

The mechanism doesn't know how to stop. It was put here long ago when we needed things. It doesn't know how to stop.

That's why I'm awake. As if something needed me.

I can understand tents. A great idea—we need tents.

Find a strong sharp thing—tiger's whisker, pine needle—and sinew. Figure out how to thread the sinew, pierce your skins. Make one long skin; you don't want gaps, you don't want rain coming in. Puncture the skin with the needle, pull the sinew through, make your sutures.

Sleep soundly in your tent, sparky brain. Tomorrow the long list of needs and inventions, needs and inventions.

It'll go on forever, drip, drip. You know that. You know that. No matter what you invent, you're useless against it.

NOVEL CHRONICLE

None of the characters wants to be in the novel. They can't act on their own, refute, correct, refuse.

Press down on the page, write a life on the monitor, imagine it's yours. Any more than a period, a question mark, a comma, a dash. The sound of a keyboard, a spark.

Tic marks on the wall. Counting the days.

LIKE CHRONICLE II

I was still not me but *like* me.

It was hard to find a job this way; I was always late.

Then a branch hit the night-lit window. (The wind made it.)

A mirror image: I wouldn't be *that* again.

SOUP CAN CHRONICLE

Of *course* these things aren't original. They've been copied since forever.

Why make them?

To think something's unique, irreplaceable: a selfish thought.

There seem to be differences, but that's just blindness.

Eternal patterns, eternal blindness.

MUSEUM CHRONICLE

1.
The thick penis of the heavy man. I've come to see if it'll move.

2.
A camera blows a person to bits, bits become stars, stars form a constellation in the shape of an eye.

3.
She took the mood of her time and put it outside. Why should everything fit in a museum?

4.
I'll mention the womb she made, birth, a TV screen from the late century, nothing's on but war, they'd signed off.

5.
The materials erase him. The ants do what they do, just like stars, constellations, little charlie chaplins, little text clusters. A percolator takes off for outer space. A penis goes too.

6.
I sit, stand, find another seat, stay still, watch, look at notes, smell a person, sit, stand.

7.
Museum guard: *Do not stick your head in there please.*

★

8.

You want the view from above, tenderly watching people in the sunny garden. You certainly wouldn't want to be down there, watched by who you really are.

9.

They totter, they're in wheelchairs, they're bored, a head's down in sleep, they're young, they kiss, they watch the fountain.

10.

A fountain repeats itself.

11.

It wouldn't burn. Flame retardant paper. Didn't I like the image I'd made? (I was relieved it hadn't burned.) It was false. As yesterday and tomorrow.

12.

As translating myself to myself.

CHRONIC CHRONICLE

I can't kill it. Organs, viscera, ideas, interior things—when they go,
I won't have done it.

You don't have to look hard to see what's in my brain.

To be heard. To be still.

The trick is to seem native. Effortless, entitled. To be an insider,
and good luck.

Chronos, Paralipomenon, things recurrent, things left out.
I'm out in the neighborhood, reading a sign for a garage sale.
Today! We're moving! A contingent walks by, whooping and
hollering, to the park. A lazy day.

I'm on a bench with my notebook, no idea where this is going.

On and on, a beautiful afternoon. Only some idea of fixity.

CHRONIC FATIGUE CHRONICLE

How can I pretend I've never written? Tried various tricks like this one.

I'm waiting for the 'ping' that means I like something.

I used to like healers. Each spark is a spark, they said, and the next spark and the next. Even the wearing down of sparks: everything's good. You should like it.

Who likes being told what to do? I'm surprised the sparks aren't self-conscious. Aren't they aware they're being watched?

I've come here alone to see what I like, sad or thinking or elated, not to be seen.

Something unkempt and tired, tolerating this very close examination.

UNSAVED CHRONICLE

A subway sign I thought said *Not only is it unsafe, it is highly hypnotic to walk between the cars.*

Or the mixology above the skyline. A lake and a land finding out as they go.

All I can say is, it looks animalistic, a big fat sunny day barreling through. This is before something happens, before the *got it.*

Signs, for example. No one should plan on them.

A story I read in a museum. Girls in Southwest Alaska drawing pictures in snow or mud to illustrate stories they'd told one another. Then their fathers looking at the ground and carving their stories onto bone knives. Story knives.

Then the story knives lost to a museum, lost fathers, lost girls, how I was taught by example not to say anything, it wouldn't be saved.

Snow, mud, the less durable parts of animals.

At most once.

III/   TECHNOPASTORAL

SCENE

A wild and desolate region; …thickets, rocks and a single tree…

EUELPIDES

<to his jay>

Do you think I should walk straight for that tree?

PISTHETÆRUS

<to his crow>

Cursed beast, what are you croaking to me?

…to retrace my steps?

—Aristophanes

HOME LIGHT

Home, a platform, thins out—
Light   *<phosphorus–Lucifer–Light Bringer–plasma>*
Plays across the plays   *<edges–mergers–midways>*

Engine, help my search
Name this zone before it's spent—
Life of the present upon a threshold

Future and past's intersecting edge
Forest comes to meadow
Sand to sea

Neustonic layer   *<Earth's babyfood>*
To polymer vortex   *<a native formula goes eternal>*
Light—

You looked back, motherly
Lover of glut and reduction
Indiscriminate touch

                       <but the hapless man touched
                       nothing but yielding air>

Yielding home

                                       Ovid,
                                 Metamorphoses

DISTANT POINTS

Skimmed from the creamy thing
they thought was needed—

Permanence

Home   the word listens and tries Restore

                    It can't be grasped   it's leaking

The victim of forward motion

             the lie of it

At distant points the foreign traveler has
necessarily to fear, that the impressions
made upon him, by local and provincial
feelings and prejudices, may usurp, in his
mind that place—which should be given
only to such as are universal Value and
property records home value and

Edward Augustus Kendall, Esq.,
*Travels Through the Northern Parts of the
United States, The Years 1807 and 1808*
New York, 1809

MOTION AND PLACE

And were the Best of Us
—those whose Actions mattered Most—

to Drown in a Crowded Sea?

Were we not Fishermen in God's
Expansive Rooms, in this our

Deserv'd Circumstance?
in this New-Found Our-Land,

Our God's Worldwide
listening in?

Motion is the translation of a
body from the place it occupies to
another place. Truly, rest is a body
remaining at the same place The
place [occupied by a body] is a
part of the immense or boundless
space which constitutes the whole
world

Leonhard Euler, *Mechanica*
Germany, 1736

TECHNOPASTORAL

Platform for miniature figures, one outerboro block
      and a pocket park, muzzy analog decades found at

www.midlife.returnshome+survives=nostalgia.biz. Each link's
      so forward-looking, highspeed-connectivity-like,
      bravura newest

satellite views hyped onscreen. I've just to adjust the language,
      navigate webplastic.lightguts, download this intersection—

and memory is memory-was. Concrete urns
      limning an overpass, pizza fronts, workaday bars,

signs for the famed stadium, bitsy lives like mine
      rounded with a snooze. Traffic snarls a powerless sky,

transient hotel façade's granted landmark status, the park's named
      Joyce Kilmer—bygone soul for such progressive
      applications!

The place zeroes and ones, and I place it—or I'm *loster*
      than time and won't be found 'til I'm a pulse, a one, a pause,
      a no....

I think that I shall never see—O
      where have all the server tools gone,

root node hidden in the tree view?
      I'll have a *banana cream squirrel* because I loved

the sound of it, *damned emotional cripple* because I love
        the sound, like code in the margins *tragic*

with errors. What'd I think I was, a poem as lovely as a tree?
        I refreshed and resurfaced with the crossing guard

in a Camelotty era—so remind me, dear browser of
        Ephemeris Time, search-engine 'crossing guard' and
        'Dodge

Coronet,' the 'Then' mothers spent in bed, postpartumly
        sewing clothes for school plays that collapsed in production

and elders bemoaned Pop Art, weeping for poems that friended
        trees, a loveliness I learned from rascals singing offkey

in reruns. Summer's measure of godly menfolk
        tuned their bongos and balalaikas on Dogshit Avenue,

for comfort, now I recall, a week after the hit and run
        <The hobbled boy grew up to fix cars>.

On such-and-such a date, registers showed negative balance,
        factories folded and were gone, *Dios mío, Gottenyu,*
        power outages shut

the drip and surge, sitters pinned notes to our sleeves,
        packed transistors and met up at Golden Star for chicken
        almond ding, talking class-war and tabs—.

Now a new tab gives me futuristic tropes, a portal to the real faux
        time and memory, pixie pixels on the *click-here*s

that take me away, a fool like me's harsh rasp.
        Hit save and my softwares crash.

LOVE

Daylilies, growing underground
love saltwater shade, gulf seafloor

they don little skulls

each a little gumball   eyeball

          little ifoam

              mon fleur

                mon crude oil country

              People will love it it's very very moving
              and there are...some connection"
              with the voyage of Vespucci Love Gives
              Me Hope Like Love Gives Me Hope?
              Try our other sites Love and desire [are]...
              accompanied by privation, because their
              object is lacking either in the present or
              in the future

                    Judah Abravanel (Leo Hebraeus),
                            Dialoghi d'amore
                              Portugal, 1501

OF KNOTS AND LYRICAL STATISTICS

Horace, in *Ars Poetica*:
    Let God not intervene
        unless a knot come worthy

        On *khipu*, experts hypothesize:
            The arrangement of 3 figure-8 knots
            represented 'Puruchuco'

In spoken Quecha: 'feather hat'
    Now: sprawling shantytown   Then: administrative center
        <feather in the cap, so to speak>

        Prayer shawl's 613 fringes, knotted
        per fringe: 8 threads, 5 knots =
        613 commandments

~700 known *khipu*
        to decode
            unknot

        $\geq$6 billion mathematical knots and links
        <circles in 3D Euclidean space>
        can't be undone

= the continuity
    of narrative and statistical unknowns

<The Lord is One>
<1?   0?>

language = home?
done = undone?

unintelligible first → last
unknown → unknown

"Experts 'decipher' Inca strings"
BBC News, 12th August 2005
(Peru ca. 1500)

ROOT NODE SONNET

But who could glean a seething brain—

cracked the earthenware   dirt   <yours and mine   seedling pain'd

spilling haplessly the unripen'd grain—   yours vs. mine>

you watched my speeding van—   as once from an open window

                                                                        off in a cloud of symbols and their time

Thereby silicic

and disinterred

I scrolled   root, element, meme—   True,

we'd inferred   before leaving, each as other   we want to be

and simply for that, loved.   Absent thine: language, load

distant code   proffering / suffering

time bits from the world wide woe   phonemically clicked   uniting rages

along mistaken unities   documenting temporarily   the mania for

infinite thought—   wide world alone   in loneliness caught

WITH THE SIGN o

                       o   dear abstract   IDs!
past   futurepast   fu   pa   !

1'll stop um!   says 1   or marry um
let down and up the flag   *1* come to this field *o*   the many!

o abstract many   looking back on it o   comes to a screeching
halt   *o* says *o* wash hands before you scroll o

unscroll   that body!   *<stand   state   stasis>*
    statistic!   spread over it the sheet

spreadsheet   *o*   won't you
press Esc, 1?   and not tally-
                 ho?

oh won oh won oh won oh won oh won oh won oh won oh won oh won oh won

title from Leonardo of Pisa
(Fibonacci), *Liber Abaci*
1202

FRIENDLY PAIRS

The soul—once paired?

                              Was an amicable
                              settlement reached?

                              Infinite,
                              those solitary digits flying off
                                    faster than satisfaction

                                    Since the matter of
                                    amicable numbers has
                                    occurred to my mind…

                                         Thabit,
                              Mesopotamia/Baghdad
                                         ca. 901

AGAPE

Had a job

Now this is me, feeling good
As in good and hungry

I'm not a bad person,
Said he on the R

<Clearing it with his smell>
I'm not here to rob or steal

I don't mean to drive you out

Men who lived a pious and reasonable
life wondered…how He had permitted a
woman who had suffered like a martyr …
to be ousted by a swineherd

Theophanes
on the deposition of Irene,
Empress of Rome, 802

WHAT THREE PILLARS OF SALT SANG

...time's pores
through
light digits
roots' children
tube-languaged

lithium'ed

electric-showered

what will win's
unknown
winning
nothing known

and though
no knowing's used
all the known
will lose

This ... made Agaz
for his fathers
who
have carried off
the youth of ...

... as well as of

right column:
from an inscription on an
Aksumite-era stele
(oldest known example
of the Ge'ez language)
Matara, Eritrea, ca. 300

CABLE

MEANT TO WRITE SOONER STOP IS FATIGUE
CONQUERING WONDERFUL US STOP IS SOMEONE
ELSES DESPERATION SLOWING DOWN THE RAM
STOP DO REPLY

For even a powerful arrow at the
end of its flight can't penetrate a
silk cloth

Zhuge Liange, advisor
to northern warlord Cao Cao,
Battle of Red Cliffs, China, 208

HIT SEND

…these verses…weren't written in my garden…
or while you, my familiar couch, supported me

. . .

this garden has hardness
this couch, no color
these verses don't depend upon
my being in this room, the water

. . .

I'm tossed on the stormy deep…
and the paper itself exposed to the dark waters

. . .

and the going-backwards machine
finds expression in its salty language:
I'll give you everything-nothing

. . .

Let the storm defeat the man!
Yet at the same time
let him halt the music of his songs
as I do mine
as the machine sings
of-self not-self!

You will go, my little book, without me to the city, but I don't envy you. Go on—
go

no self no past no self no past no past no past no self no past no self

Ovid (in exile),
Tristia
10 AD

A YELLOW DWARF'S PHOTONEGATIVE CAPABILITY

The zooplanktons come to shore to wake me. I know what they want—we share a history. I *know*. They trail me to the sea, and I set our polymers on the tide. We drink. We float. I return to shore. They follow me and wait for something more.

carbon-based   *carbon-based synthetics*

So I only *thought* I knew what the zooplanktons wanted. But if I'd written, *We share a history therefore I* think *I know*, that would've been inaccurate. Hindsight. *I know what they want* is the accurate statement—but *know* is an inaccurate word. *Know* should express the not-knowing. The omniscient not-known.

Training black bears, grizzly bears,
foxes, panthers, lynxes and tigers,
he, with their aid, fought with
Blazing God in the desert

Sima Qian, *Records of the Grand Historian* (begun
while he was imprisoned),
Han Dynasty ca. 91 BC

SEARCH RAP

tree shaken   sweet for sampling
you taste what's fallen <*you hungry felon*>
apple-bitten and taken:
who decided you shouldn't thrive?
your <*runtime*> engine's loading
self-loathing and accusation <*despairation*>
so you stop searching there
stop sampling the live sensation
and a keyword entered one sec ago <*unslowed*>
searches for <*idealthen*>
<*language-fix-me*> as though
<*presplit*><*prebinary*> pre-eden-eden
could sample itself <hi. who posted this?>
<*source*> searching for <*source*>
<*source*> searching

GLEANING

Sign 11   'skyband/throne'
Sign 22   'mat'
Script death

Scriptual silence   hydrous
magnesium silicate   green-mottled
world-poor serpentine   writing to itself

[X]'s mannequins use facial recognition software
that can't be read, to glean customer
demographic data and shopping patterns

Be quiet, we said,
which didn't mean
we understood

Olmec glyphs (likely the earliest
writing system in the Americas)
from the Cascajal Block,
Mexico, ca. 900 BC

businessweek.com
print advertisement posted on
the Long Island Rail Road,
New York, ca. 2015

SEQUENCE
<a selfie>

Quarkish. On-offish. ATCAATTAAAATTTTATGTGAish. Hello-goodbye-ish. Code-switchily in thrall to little protein bits like Big Bang's in thrall to like a black hole's in thrall to my birthplace seen from their distance *slush slosh now waterways grasslands now pasture now wood and cloth sails a haarlem river now steamships traffic to a stadium spilling onto the overhead pass now* code mad with travel sending stop-go symbols alluring wet-for-hard-for an epidemic transmitting-detecting home-none gone-here

01001001 00100000 01000001
01101101 00100000 01010100
01101000 01100001 01110100

SOURCES AND NOTES

Poems in Sections I and III sample or refer to text from Internet search engines, websites, and print sources. Some of these are:

In 'Breaking Down': lines from 'After the death of the Emperor Temmu,' a waka, ca. 703, attributed to Empress Jitō (Unonosarara), 41st emperor of Japan. In *Kokka Taikan*, Book II, 1901, and on wikipedia.org.

In 'Night': *What was there to complain of...* and *The grief-stricken birds...flinty rocks and the woods.* From *The Metamorphoses of Ovid,* Book X, translated by Mary M. Innes. Penguin Books Ltd., 1955.

In '@Work': *pictograph barley...*, *cuneiform barley...*, and *this tablet records a quantity of barley*. From "The development of writing," mesopotamia.co.uk.

In 'Plasma: anything formed': the definition of plasma is from *A Greek-English Lexicon*, Henry George Liddell and Robert Scott. At perseus.tufts.edu.

'Home Light' includes excerpts from the myth of Orpheus in *The Metamorphoses of Ovid*, Books X and XI, ibid.

In 'Hit Send': *...these verses...supported me, I'm tossed... dark waters, Let the storm...as I do mine,* and *You will go, my little book...Go on—go*. From Ovid's *Tristia*, Book II.XI:44, translated by A.S. Kline, 2003. At tkline.freeserve.co.uk.

'Sequence<a selfie>' contains (1) a miniscule section of the Homo sapiens forkhead box P2 gene sequence (the so-called "language gene"), on ncbi.nlm.nih.gov/projects; and (2) binary code for I Am That, using binarytranslator.com.

In 'If Then,' *immen, tarsa,* and *tersesthai* are Sumerian, Sanskrit, and Greek for 'thirst.'

In 'Like Chronicle,' the question "What is it like to be a bat?" is Thomas Nagel's, from his essay by that title in *The Philosophical Review,* 1974.

'Ax Chronicle' contains a brief quotation from *The Brothers Karamazov* by Fyodor Dostoyevsky, translated by David McDuff. Penguin Books, 1993.

The epigraph for Section III ('Technopastoral') is from Aristophanes' *Birds* in *The Complete Greek Drama,* vol. 2, Eugene O'Neill, Jr. Random House, 1938.

ACKNOWLEDGEMENTS

Work in this collection has appeared previously,
and in earlier versions, in the *Dusie Blog*, *Exposition Review*,
The Prose-Poem Project (print and digital editions), *The Southampton
Review*, *Touch the Donkey*, *Tupelo Quarterly* and *Yellow Field*.
'Chronicles' was published as a 100-edition fine art chapbook
by PressBoardPress (Buffalo and Syracuse, New York, 2013).
Additionally, 'Motion and Place' was reconceived as a video poem
for Counterpath Press's 'Open Opening,' Denver, Colorado, 2016.
Heartfelt thanks to the editors and curators of these publications
and venues.

The author also acknowledges the support of a Faculty
Development & Research Grant from Hofstra University,
especially as the grant was awarded to enable completion of a novel
but resulted in the completion of this decidedly hybrid work.